YOUNG RESEARCHER

THE VIKINGS

Hazel Mary Martell

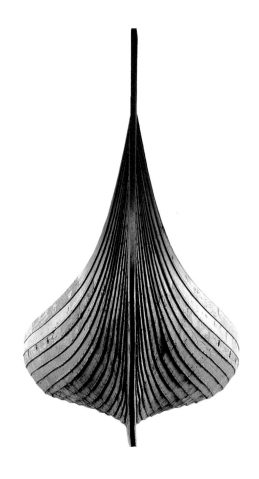

HEINEMANN

HEINEMANN EDUCATIONAL
a division of Heinemann Educational Books Ltd
Halley Court, Jordan Hill, Oxford OX2 8EJ

OXFORD LONDON EDINBURGH MADRID
ATHENS BOLOGNA PARIS MELBOURNE
SYDNEY AUCKLAND SINGAPORE TOKYO
IBADAN NAIROBI HARARE GABORONE
PORTSMOUTH NH (USA)

ISBN 0 431 00564 8

British Library Cataloguing in Publication Data
Martell, Hazell Mary
    The Vikings
    1. Vikings
    I. Title II. Series
    948'.02

Designed by Julian Holland Publishing Ltd
Colour artwork by Martin Smillie
Picture research by Faith Perkins
Editorial planning by Jackie Gaff

Printed in Hong Kong

92 93 94 95 96 10 9 8 7 6 5 4 3 2

Photographic acknowledgements
The author and publishers wish to acknowledge, with
thanks, the following photographic sources:
a = above b = below l = left r = right
Arnamagneaan Institute, Reykjavik p11; A.T.A. Stockholm
pp9, 14, 49, 57; ARXIU-MAS, Barcelona p52; Bibliothek der
Rijksuniversiteit, Utrecht p53; Copenhagen University p27*b*;
C. M. Dixon pptitle, 5*a*, 81*l* and *r*, 10, 13, 15*a*, 17*a* and *b*, 18,
20*a*, 21, 25*a*, 27*a*, 29, 32, 33*b*, 42, 47*a*, 48, 56, 58; Werner
Forman Archive title page pp12 (Statens Historiska Museet,
Stockholm), 15*b* (National Museum of Iceland), 16*a* (Statens
Historiska Museet, Stockholm), 16*b* (Manz Museum), 26
(National Museum, Copenhagen), 35*b* (Statens Historiska
Museet, Stockholm), 59*a* and cover and *b*; Robert Harding
Photograph Library pp45, 54*b*; Historiska Museet,
Stockholm p30; Michael Holford pp20*b*, 28; Kungl
Biblioteket, Stockholm p44; National Museet, Copenhagen
pp24, 43*b*; National Museum of Ireland p51; Roskilde
Museum, Denmark p7*a*; Scottish Tourist Board pp19, 50;
Stofnun Arna Magnussonar, Reykjavik p54*a*; University
Museum of National Antiquities, Oslo pp5*b* (photograph
Eirik I Johnsen); 23*a*, 25*b*, 33*a*, 37*a* and *b*, 39 and cover 43*a*
and cover and *b*; Weidenfeld and Nicolson Archive 51, 57;
York Archaeological Trust pp6, 7*b*, 22, 23*b*, 36*b*.
The publishers have made every effort to trace the
copyright holders, but if they have inadvertently
overlooked any, they will be pleased to make the necessary
arrangement at the first opportunity.

Note to the reader
In this book there are some words in the text which are printed in **bold** type. This shows that the word is listed in
the glossary on page 62. The glossary gives a brief explanation of words which may be new to you.

Contents

Who were the Vikings?

The Vikings lived in north east Europe over a thousand years ago. They were a group of people who came from the countries we now call Norway, Denmark and Sweden. A very old history book, *The Anglo-Saxon Chronicle*, tells us that the first Vikings came to England in the year AD 789. The book was written nearly 100 years later, when Alfred was king of England. The book also describes Alfred's battles against the Vikings.

At first, these people were known as Norsemen, or Danes. These were the words they used in their own languages. Norse was a Norwegian word for 'north'. The word 'viking' was used to describe what these people did. It meant something like 'to go across the seas'. This word was soon used to describe the people too.

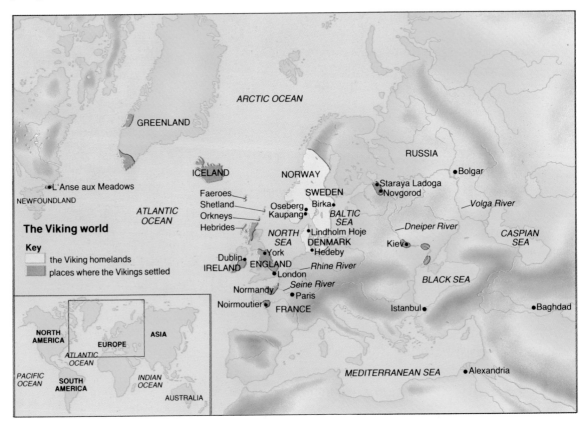

The Viking world

Key

☐ the Viking homelands
▨ places where the Vikings settled

Viking is an Old English word for a pirate which was how the people of Europe thought of the Vikings from about AD 789. This was because the Vikings attacked **monasteries** in Europe, and stole the treasures. They took away the **monks** who lived and prayed there, and sold them as slaves in Arab markets in the east in return for silver. The Vikings also attacked cities, like Paris and London. The nursery rhyme 'London Bridge is Falling Down' is about an attack by Vikings led by Olaf the Stout. He and his men rowed up the River Thames and fastened ropes to the wooden bridge. Then they rowed away as fast as they could, pulling the bridge down as they went.

Today, however, as historians find out more about the Vikings a different picture of their life can be formed. Evidence now shows that they were also farmers and **traders**. They told stories which have become famous. These stories have been printed in books and are still read today.

The trading journeys

The Vikings' ship-building skills made it possible for them to go on long journeys. Vikings from Norway travelled across the Atlantic Ocean to Iceland, Greenland and North America. Danish Vikings settled in France and England. Other Vikings from Sweden travelled into Russia and along the rivers. From trading cities like Kiev on the Dnieper River, and Bolgar on the Volga River, they went on to the Black Sea and the Caspian Sea and the cities of Istanbul and Baghdad. Ships were so important to the Vikings that some dead kings and queens were buried in ships. Altogether the Viking Age lasted about 300 years. By 1100 the great adventures were over and most of the Vikings were living in peace with their neighbours.

△ ▽ The Vikings were skilled carvers of stone and wood. They also made jewellery from bronze and silver. Animal shapes were very popular in Viking art. The animals usually had long, ribbon-like bodies which twisted around each other, like the animal and snake in this silver brooch from Lindholm Hoje in Denmark. The animal head carved on a wooden post was found in a ship burial at Oseberg in Norway.

How we know about the Vikings

Much of what we know about the Vikings comes from evidence uncovered by **archaeologists.** They dig at different sites where they hope to find objects which the Vikings used. By studying these objects, or **artefacts,** and the places where they are found, archaeologists build up a picture of what life was like in the past. Many of these digs, or **excavations,** have been in the Vikings' homelands. Others have been in places the Vikings went to as **raiders,** traders and **settlers.**

Not all sites are easy to excavate. Many have been built over since the Viking Age. Archaeologists can only work on these when more recent buildings are knocked down. Then they have to work quickly before the site is used again for another building.

Some sites were abandoned by the Vikings,

◁ Archaeologists at work at Coppergate, York, in 1979. This English Viking site is between the Ouse and Foss Rivers. The soil was damp and this helped to preserve many Viking Age artefacts beneath more recent buildings. Excavation revealed the remains of four rows of timber houses and workshops. Some walls were still standing up to one metre high. In and around these buildings, archaeologists found over 30 000 objects. People who had lived and worked there had lost these things or thrown them away. They included glass beads, amber pendants, metal brooches, knives, keys and coins. There were also leather boots and shoes, and wooden cups and spoons made by the woodworkers, or coopers, from whom Coppergate got its name.

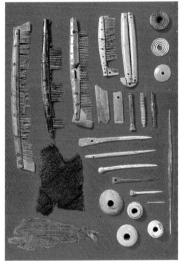

◁ An underwater excavation at Roskilde, Denmark. In 1956, part of a Viking ship was found in the shallow water. A dam was built around the ship in 1962, and the water was drained out. Excavation of the site revealed the timbers of five ships. They had been filled with stones and sunk on purpose to prevent Harald Hardradi reaching the town of Roskilde by boat. The water had made the timbers soft, but they were raised and conserved. Then they were re-moulded to their original shapes and are now displayed in the Roskilde Museum.

however, and now lie under farmland. One of these is Hedeby in Denmark, a famous market town in the Viking Age. In 1049 it was burned down by Harald Hardradi, king of Norway. Less than 20 years later, the town was attacked again and it was never rebuilt after that. Excavation began in 1953 and revealed the remains of the old town. The harbour was also excavated. It had been protected by a high wooden fence, or **stockade,** and at its entrance part of a Viking ship was found. This had been on fire when it sank at the time of Harald Hardradi's attack.

Looking for artefacts is just part of an archaeologist's work. For an accurate picture of Viking life, all finds must be recorded. Objects which cannot be moved, such as stone foundations of buildings, are measured and photographed. Smaller finds, such as coins, jewellery, leather, cloth and timbers, are cleaned and preserved. Soil samples are also studied. In these are found the remains of seeds, insects and animal bones, which all help to show what conditions were like on the site in Viking times.

△ A selection of finds excavated by archaeologists. The combs were made from deer antlers and the pins were made from animal bones. Even the small scraps of cloth are of value to the archaeologist who can study them in a laboratory to find out what they were made of, how they were woven and what dyes were used to colour them.

Evidence in pictures and words

Some clues of Viking life come from cloth pictures, or **tapestries,** made in the Viking Age. One of these tapestries was found in the ship burial at Oseberg. It has now been restored and shows the type of clothes the Vikings wore and the transport they used on land. Farming and ship-building methods are shown on the Bayeux Tapestry. This tells the story of the **conquest** of England in 1066 by the Normans from France. Vikings had settled in northern France 100 years before.

Other clues come from carvings in wood or stone. Often these not only tell a story, but also show something of Viking life. For instance, carvings at

◁ ▷ Woodcarvings from the church at Hylestad, Norway. They tell the story of Sigurd the Dragon-slayer, whose adventures were very popular with the Vikings. At the bottom right, two Viking warriors, Sigurd and Reginn, are making a sword called Gram. Above this, Gram breaks when the sword is tested for strength. After Gram has been mended, Sigurd uses it to kill the dragon which guarded some treasure. At the bottom left, Reginn watches Sigurd roast the dragon's heart over a fire. Sigurd burns his thumb and sucks it, tasting the dragon's blood. This lets him understand two birds singing in the tree above him. They tell him that Reginn plans to steal the dragon's treasure. Sigurd then kills Reginn with his sword. The picture at the top left shows Gunnar, Sigurd's brother-in-law. He has killed Sigurd and stolen the treasure, but has been thrown into a snake-pit for not telling where he has hidden it. As he dies, he plays the harp with his toes.

Runes
Some of our knowledge of the Vikings comes from inscriptions made in runes. These shapes or letters had straight lines which could be carved into wood, stone or metal. At first they were thought to be magic. For example, runes carved on a sword were thought to make it stronger. Later they were used on memorial stones. The picture on the memorial stone at Ramsund, Sweden (left) is from the Sigurd legend. The runes are carved in the dragon's body but they are not about the story. The letters say, 'Sigrid built this bridge in memory of her husband, Holmger. (She) was Orm's daughter.' Runes were known as *futhark* from the names of the first six runes. There were only 16 runes altogether. This meant there was not a rune for every sound in the language and so spelling was not easy for the rune carver.

Hylestad church, Norway, show a sword being made and meat being cooked. Other carvings include pictures of ships in full sail and men fishing. Stone carvings often also have messages cut in **runes,** which are the stick-like letters the Vikings used for writing.

Clues in words

A Viking could only write something down by carving runes into stone or wood. This took a long time even for a short message. Stories, poems and history were learned by heart and passed on. By the end of the twelfth century, however, the Vikings in Iceland began to write in ink on calf-skin, or **vellum.** This was much quicker, so now they could write down histories, such as the *Landnamabok.* This told of the first 400 settlers in Iceland and the land they claimed. Later, the Icelandic **sagas,** or stories, were written down and enjoyed by everyone. They told of Viking Age adventures and were copied out time after time.

Other people also wrote about the Vikings. An Arab trader, Ibn Fadlan, tells of the Vikings he met in Russia. Another Arab trader, Al-Tattushi, visited Hedeby, in Denmark, and wrote about what he saw there.

Society and government

Viking society was divided into three groups. The people at the top were called *jarls*. The *jarls* were rich landowners and were generous to their friends and followers. They were also powerful. As more people began to live closer together, the local *jarl* was usually chosen as the leader. As time went on one *jarl* would become more powerful than the others in a district. He might even become known as king. He was only king in his own district, however, and did not rule the whole country.

The largest group in Viking society was the *karls*. They were freeborn men and usually owned land. When a *karl* died, his land went to his eldest son. This left younger sons with no land of their own. They were still *karls,* however, and often worked for other *karls* until they could buy their own land.

The slaves, or *thralls,* owned nothing and had no rights. Children of *thralls* grew up to be *thralls* themselves. Prisoners taken in battle could also become *thralls.* If a *karl* was very poor, had no family to help him and had no land on which to grow food, he could also volunteer to become a *thrall.* When this happened, he lost all the rights he had had as a *karl.* It was possible for a *thrall* to work very hard and buy freedom for himself and his family.

Government by discussion

In Viking society open-air meetings of free men were called to settle disputes and discuss problems. These meetings were called *Things.* Each *Thing* had its own set of laws. As kings became more powerful, the *Things* in Norway, Denmark and Sweden still dealt with local problems. These included such matters as divorce, theft and land ownership.

Iceland never had a king, however. Instead its people were governed by a national *Thing,* as well as by local *Things.* The national *Thing* was called the

△ Tynwald Hill in the Isle of Man. The name Tynwald is from the Norse words *thing,* or parliament, and *vellir* which means a field. The Viking *Thing* met in a field here every summer to settle disputes. The parliament of the Isle of Man still meets at Tynwald Hill once a year, on Old Midsummer Day. Laws passed in the last year are read out.

Written evidence from Iceland shows that the meetings of *Things* were great social events, too. Although only the men could vote, they often took their families with them. People wore their best clothes. Merchants set up booths and traded there. News was exchanged and marriages arranged.

Althing and met for two weeks at midsummer each year. This was because it was easier for people to travel in summer. The *Althing* was held at a place called *Thingvellir*. The free men came from all over Iceland to listen to the Law Speaker. He recited the law codes which governed them. Most Vikings respected these laws. A Viking who would not accept the ruling of the *Althing* became an outlaw. He had to give up his belongings and his land. Then he had to flee the country, as anyone could kill an outlaw without punishment.

△ An illustration from *Harald Finehair's Saga*. When Harald Finehair's father died, Harald inherited the kingdom of Vestfold. At that time Norway was made up of many little kingdoms, but Harald wanted to rule over them all. To do this he made an ally of *jarl* Hakon, who ruled over the far north. They joined forces and fought their way south. They defeated the last of their enemies at the battle of Hafrsfjord in about 890. Harald was the first king to rule over Norway.

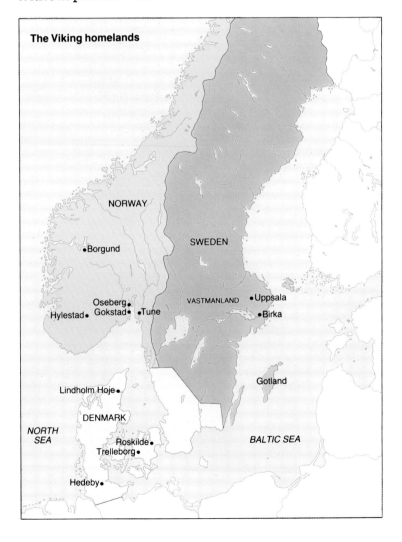

The Viking homelands

NORWAY

Borgund

SWEDEN

Oseberg
Hylestad• Gokstad• •Tune

VASTMANLAND •Uppsala
•Birka

Gotland

Lindholm Hoje•

DENMARK

NORTH
SEA

Roskilde•
Trelleborg•

BALTIC SEA

Hedeby•

◁ During the Viking Age the boundaries between the three countries were not as firmly fixed as they are now. Denmark included parts of what are now Germany and Sweden. People lived mainly where the land was fertile, so large areas had nobody living in them.

Clothes and appearance

We have many clues about the Vikings' appearance. Some are in pictures carved on stones. A whole series of carved and painted stones has been found on the island of Gotland. Other pictures are **embroidered** on tapestries. There are also written descriptions in the sagas. One king gave his men this advice: 'Wear long cloth trousers of brown or any colour other than scarlet. Wear brown, green or red **tunics** of good quality cloth.' He also told them to take care of their beards and their hair.

Women dressed simply most of the time. They wore an ankle-length dress made of linen. Linen is fine cloth woven with threads from the stem of a plant. This simple dress, or **shift,** was usually pleated and fastened at the neck with a drawstring. Over this shift Viking women wore a woollen tunic. This was in two pieces, held together with straps over the shoulders. These straps were fastened to the tunic by brooches. Rows of beads were hung between these brooches. A chain hanging down from one of the brooches held a knife, a comb, a key and a case of needles.

Both men and women wore flat leather shoes. They also wore cloaks in cold weather. The women fastened theirs with a brooch in the middle of the chest. The men, however, fastened theirs with a brooch high on one shoulder. Rings and bracelets were worn by men as well as women. Silver jewellery was also a form of money. Pieces could be cut off and used to pay for goods.

Most clothes were made at home by the Viking women who also made most of the cloth. For special occasions, however, they wore silks from China. Viking traders bought these silks, and **brocades** with patterns in gold and silver thread, at markets in the east. Sometimes strips of silk were embroidered with gold thread and used to trim cuffs and hems. Men also used silk headbands to hold back their hair. When

△ This Viking-Age pendant from Sweden gives direct evidence of a woman's appearance. Her trailing dress is pleated at the back and over it she wears a shawl. Her long hair falls loosely from a knot at the back of her head. The beads on her chest probably hang from her shoulder-brooches.

◁ These are the sort of clothes a Viking farmer and his wife would have worn. They dressed to be comfortable, not fashionable. That was why styles did not change much throughout the whole Viking period.

Al-Tattushi visited Hedeby, he wrote that both men and women wore make-up on their eyes.

Cloth rots after many years, but small pieces of it have been found in some Viking graves. These pieces have been examined in laboratories, and archaeologists have found that they were dyed in bright colours. Vegetable dyes such as woad and madder were used to give blue and red cloth. Other colours included green, brown, black and yellow from earth and plants.

△ Metal brooches were worn by all Viking women. An oval brooch, like this one, was worn on each shoulder, to hold the loops of the tunic. Smaller brooches would be used to fasten the shawl or cloak.

Family life

The family was very important to the Vikings. It included not only parents and children, but also uncles and aunts and distant cousins. Members of a family were usually more loyal to each other than they were to their leaders. This loyalty sometimes led to quarrels, or **feuds,** between families. These feuds could last for two or three generations. In *Egil's Saga,* a feud between Egil's father and Harald Finehair lasts until the time of their grandchildren. A feud usually started because a member of one family killed a member of another. The dead man's family then took revenge. Instead of killing the killer, however, they usually killed another member of his family. This led to more killings. Sometimes feuds were taken to the *Thing.* There it was decided who was in the wrong and that person and his family had to give land or money to the other family, to make up for the wrong.

Marriage and divorce

Whether they were married or not, Viking women were treated with respect. They were allowed to choose their own husbands and keep their own property after they were married. When their husbands were away raiding or trading, the women were in charge of the house. They could then take decisions and make bargains on behalf of their husbands.

Marriages often took place in the early winter, when everyone was at home. After the **ceremony** the feasting sometimes lasted for a fortnight. The Vikings could get a divorce. To make this legal, the husband or wife had to make a formal speech in front of witnesses. Some of their reasons seem very unimportant today. For example, one man divorced his wife because she wore trousers. A woman divorced her husband for showing too much bare chest.

△ This rune-stone from Vastmanland, Sweden, was carved nearly 1000 years ago. A farmer from Hassmyra had it made in memory of his wife, Odindisa. One sentence reads, 'No better wife will come to Hassmyra to look after the farm'. Another good wife was Bergthora in *Njal's Saga.* Her husband was caught up in a feud with another family. Their house had been set on fire, but Bergthora refused the chance to escape. She stayed with her husband, saying, 'I was married young to Njal and I promised him that one fate shall fall on us both'.

Children

When a baby was born, its father accepted it into his family by picking up the baby and wrapping it in his cloak. If the baby was badly deformed or very weak, however, the father would not do this. The baby would then be left to die.

Small children lived at home with their parents. Older children were sometimes fostered out. This was especially true for boys. Ties with foster families were often as strong as ties with natural families. This was very useful if a Viking was caught up in a feud or any sort of a dispute. His foster family might help him if his own family could not.

As soon as they were old enough, children started to learn the skills they would need for the rest of their lives. Girls learned to cook, spin, weave cloth and sew. They also learned how to milk the cows and make butter and cheese. They helped to weed the fields and look after the animals. The boys learned how to hunt and fish, to tan leather and do other jobs around the farm. Both girls and boys learned how to ride, to swim and to handle weapons. Sometimes this was done as a game using toy swords made of wood.

△ This carved whalebone plaque is from the grave of a rich Viking woman in Norway. Several others have also been found, but no one is quite certain what they were for. It is possible that these whalebones were used as ironing-boards for linen garments. A round glass object would be used to smooth out the seams. The plaque might also have been used for pleating linen. This would be done by folding the cloth while it was wet and then wrapping it around the plaque to dry.

◁ The Vikings enjoyed board games. One game was called *hnefatafl*. Among playing pieces for this was a 'king' who had to be protected by his men against an attack from the men belonging to the other player.

The Viking gods

The Vikings believed in many gods and goddesses. These were members of two families, called the Asar and the Vanir. Both families lived in a place called Asgard and had once been at war with each other.

The earth, where people lived, was called Midgard. Asgard was joined to Midgard by a rainbow bridge, known as Bifrost. Around Midgard, was a deep ocean full of monsters. Beyond this ocean was Utgard where the Frost Giants lived. These giants were enemies of the gods and one day would destroy them at a battle called Ragnarok. Underneath these worlds of gods, people and giants was Niflheim which was full of ice and mist. Vikings thought they would go there if they died in bed.

If Vikings died in battle, however, they went to **Valhalla.** This was the great hall in Asgard, belonging to Odin who was the greatest of the Viking gods. Women called Valkyries took the dead from the battlefield to Valhalla. Odin needed these brave fighters to help him in his battle against the giants. He brought them to life again. Every day 'they went out into the enclosure and fought and "killed" each other. Then in the evening, they rode home to Valhalla to eat and drink'.

The journey to the after-life

Many Vikings thought that a person's spirit sailed off to a new life after death. This is why kings and queens were often buried in a ship, along with their possessions and food for the journey. Archaeologists have found other evidence of Vikings' beliefs. Many ordinary people had stones set around their graves in the shape of a ship. Other Vikings believed that the dead came to life again in their grave-mounds and so they buried dead people with food and useful objects.

△ A silver charm in the shape of Thor's hammer. Many Vikings believed that evil giants and dwarfs lived in mountains and rocky places and so Vikings wore these charms to protect themselves.

△ This carved stone from Kirk Andreas in the Isle of Man shows a scene from the legend of Ragnarok or Doom of the Gods. Odin, with his raven and his spear, is being attacked and eaten by the grey wolf, Fenrir.

Odin, Thor and Frey

Odin was the most important of the Viking gods. He was also known as Odin All-Father and belonged to the Asar family. He was thought to be aloof and mysterious. He was also very wise and had sacrificed one of his eyes to gain knowledge and understanding. He knew about the magic of the runes and was the god of poets. He was also the god of kings, jarls, chieftains and magicians. He had two pet ravens called Huginn and Muninn. These names mean Thought and Memory. Every day the ravens would fly all over the world, then return to Odin at night to tell him what they had seen. He also had an eight-legged horse called Sleipnir and two wolves which went hunting with him at night. Odin's wife was called Frigg and they had a son called Baldr who was both handsome and friendly. Baldr was also a god, but he was accidentally killed by his brother who was blind.

Thor also belonged to the Asar family. He was the most popular of all the Viking gods. He was large and had a bright red beard. He was quick-tempered, but soon calmed down again. He also liked to laugh and was very strong. He had a chariot pulled by goats. When he rode across the sky in this chariot, the thunder rumbled. He had a hammer called Mjöllni and he used this in some of his battles with the giants. He was not cunning like Odin and was often in danger of losing the fight with the giants, but he would keep on struggling until he won. The Viking farmers and their families liked telling stories of Thor's adventures and sometimes they would invent new stories, too. One favourite tells of him stealing a large cauldron of beer from the giants so that the gods can have a party.

Frey was the other popular Viking god. He and his twin sister, Freyja, belonged to the Vanir family. He was the god of love and marriage. He also ruled the rain and the sunshine which made crops grow. He was most popular in Sweden, but he was also worshipped in Norway and Iceland. Although no Viking temple has yet been found, a monk called Adam of Bremen, in north Germany, described a temple at Uppsala in Sweden in the eleventh century. Its roof was covered in gold and inside there were statues of Odin, Thor and Frey.

△ Thor, the Viking god of thunder. This bronze statuette was found in Iceland.

Living on the land

Most Vikings were farmers and spent a lot of time working on their land. For food the Vikings kept cattle, sheep, goats, pigs and hens. These also provided skins, leather and wool for clothes and household goods. Near the house they grew vegetables such as cabbages and onions. Archaeologists have found traces of apples, so there was probably also an orchard with apple trees. Beyond this were fields of oats, barley, wheat or rye. These fields were usually enclosed with stone walls to keep the animals out. Grass was cut and dried to make hay to feed the animals in winter.

Much of this information is from sagas and from excavations. Some Viking farms are now completely overgrown, but photographs from the air can show the patterns of old fields and buildings which cannot be seen from the ground. In Norway, Denmark and Sweden, however, most Viking farms were on good land and are still farms today. This means that most archaeological evidence is from places such as Iceland. There, some farms were abandoned in the Viking Age and never lived in again.

Wherever they were, however, the Viking farms were built to a similar plan. The main building in each one was the **longhouse.** This was oblong in shape

◁ In Iceland, wood and stone were scarce and so houses were built of blocks of grass and earth cut from the fields. This turf was also used for the roofs. The grass kept growing. The layer of turf kept cold air out and trapped warm air inside the house in winter.

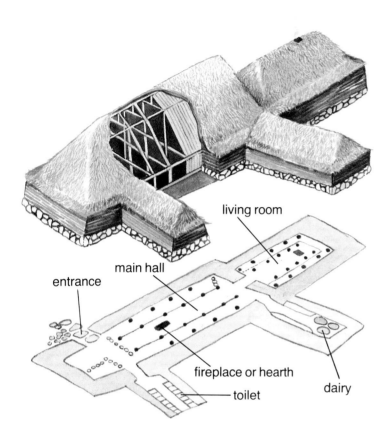

living room

main hall

entrance

fireplace or hearth

toilet

dairy

◁ The plan of a farmhouse at Stöng, Iceland. The original farmhouse was abandoned around 1104 when a nearby volcano erupted and covered the farm in ash. In 1939, the site was excavated to reveal the plan of the house. The farmhouse was rebuilt nearby, based on this plan and other archaeological evidence.

▽ Archaeologists have uncovered the stone foundations of a Viking farm at Jarlshof, on the island of Shetland, in Scotland. There are very few trees on Shetland so the buildings were of stone with thatched roofs.

and up to 30 metres long. On the earliest farms, this was the only building and the farmer's family shared it with their animals. Later, more buildings were built around the longhouse. These would include a barn, or a **byre,** to shelter the animals in winter. There would be a **smithy** where iron tools were made or mended.

The Vikings had to use whatever they found nearby for their buildings. In most places there were plenty of trees, so the houses were built of wood. Others were built of stone. Roofs were **thatched** with straw or reeds. On the gables, or ends, of the houses were carved wooden boards, known as verge-boards. These stopped the wind getting under the thatch and blowing the roof off.

The farming year

On a small farm the work was done by the farmer and his family. On larger farms, they were helped by *thralls* and by other *karls* who did not have land of their own. These *karls* were usually treated as part of the family. The *thralls* did work which was dirty or heavy. For example, they spread manure on the fields and dug peat for the fires.

For everyone, however, spring was a busy time on the farm. The fields were ploughed and the seeds sown for the wheat and other grain crops. Vegetables were planted and in the south **flax** was grown for linen. The fields where grass would grow for hay were spread with manure. This had been collected from the byres while the animals were indoors in winter.

When this work was done, the farmer would probably go raiding or trading for the summer. His wife was then left in charge of the farm. She had to make sure enough hay and **fodder** crops were grown to feed the animals through the winter. In Norway especially the cattle and sheep were taken to

△ On this stone from Gotland, a man is spearing a fish from a boat. Fish were also caught in nets and traps, and fish-hooks have been found on some sites.

▽ This scene from the Bayeux Tapestry shows a farmer ploughing and sowing seeds. This tapestry is from the late Viking Age, but saga evidence and archaeology show that it gives an accurate picture of Viking farming methods.

The summer months

In Iceland most of the six months of summer were named after the work which was done on the farm at that time. They were:

Cuckoo month/sowing time – mid April to mid May
Egg time/lambs' fold time – mid May to mid June
Shieling month/sun month – mid June to mid July
Haymaking month – mid July to mid August
Corncutting month – mid August to mid September
Autumn month – mid September to mid October

△ Some of the tools made by the smiths were axes. They were made from iron and sometimes decorated with silver, bronze or brass. This axehead was found in Denmark. It is made from iron and decorated with silver.

mountain pastures, or **shielings** for the summer. This meant that the grass around the farmstead could be kept for hay.

Autumn was another busy time and the farmer would come back to work on the farm. Everyone helped to cut and harvest the crops. The corn was beaten to separate the grain. The grain was then ground up for flour or used to make beer. Not all the animals could be fed over the winter and so the weakest ones were killed. Their meat was salted, smoked or dried so it could be eaten during the winter.

Cold weather and long hours of darkness meant that not much could be done outside in winter. People on the farmstead were still kept busy, however. Hides and sheepskins from the animals killed in the autumn were turned into items such as shoes, harnesses and sleeping-bags. In the smithy, tools and equipment were made and mended. These included hammers, axes, tongs and chisels. Nails and fishing-hooks were also made, as well as weapons and kitchen utensils. The Vikings also repaired their boats at this time, ready for another year.

Inside a longhouse

The earliest longhouse had just one room in which everybody lived, ate and slept. This had a long hearth down the centre and was sometimes called a fire-hall, or *skali. Grettir's Saga* describes the inside of a *skali* in the evening. 'Men sat there by the long fires. Tables were set in front of them for their meal and afterwards they would sleep by the fires.'

Later longhouses had more rooms. There was a bedroom for the farmer and his wife and a room for the women to do their spinning and weaving. Sometimes there was also a kitchen and a dairy where food could be stored. The *skali* was still the most important room, however. There, meals were eaten and guests were entertained. Benches were built into the long walls and used as seats by day and beds by night.

Whatever the outside of the longhouse was made of, the inside walls were usually of wood. The floor was of hard-packed earth, covered with rushes. Some houses had windows which let the light in during the day. These had no glass, but shutters could

◁ This reconstruction of a Viking house in York shows how important the hearth was as a centre of family life.

be pulled across to keep out the worst draughts. The roof was held up by two rows of wooden posts and had a hole in the middle for the smoke to escape from the fire. Not all smoke escaped, however, and so it could be quite smoky and smelly inside.

In the evening some light came from the fire. The rest was from flares fixed on the walls or from little lamps. These were small bowls made out of **soapstone,** a soft rock which carves easily. These lamps held burning oil and were hung from the roof, or placed on the floor or table. Tapestries were hung on the walls for decoration and to keep out the many draughts. At bedtime, bedding was spread out on the benches. There would be mattresses filled with straw or hay, pillows and quilts filled with feathers, woollen rugs or blankets, and perhaps a sheepskin cover, too.

There were no cupboards and so food was stored in casks and tubs. Spare clothes were probably kept in chests. Some chests were found in the Oseberg ship burial. Other items were hung on pegs on the wall or simply put in a corner until they were needed.

△ This wooden bed was found on the Oseberg ship. It would have belonged to an important person because ordinary people had no beds. The animals carved on the head-posts were to frighten away evil spirits in the night.

◁ Spinning wool and weaving it into cloth were daily tasks for most Viking women. After the wool had been roughly cleaned, it was combed to make all the fibres lie the same way. Then it was attached to a distaff, which was a special wooden stick. This was held in the left hand. The wool was pulled from it gently so as not to break the fibres. The loose end was fixed to a smaller stick, called a spindle. This had a weight, or whorl, attached to the bottom. It was set spinning and, as it fell to the floor, it twisted the wool into a strong thread. This thread was often dyed before being woven into cloth on a loom.

Cooking and eating

Archaeologists have many clues from finds of bones and seeds about what the Vikings ate. At Hedeby, Denmark, seeds from raspberries, strawberries, plums and cherries were found. Fish bones from cod, haddock and herring were found at York. Bones of other animals, such as pigs and sheep, show the Vikings also ate meat. Meat was usually stewed, but sometimes it was roasted over the fire on a long-handled fork, or a **spit.** Farmers kept chickens, geese and ducks for eggs as well as meat. In the forests they hunted wild animals like deer and boar. In the north, they hunted reindeer, seals and whales. In Iceland seabirds and their eggs were also eaten.

Some food was buried in Viking graves. In the ship burial at Oseberg there were the remains of hazelnuts, cress, mustard and horseradish. The Vikings also grew garlic to flavour their food and spices were bought by traders from markets at Istanbul and Baghdad, in the east.

Their main vegetables were cabbages, onions and peas. They ate rye or barley bread and porridge was made from oatmeal and barley. Milk was drunk by itself or heated to make **curds,** a type of soft cheese, and **whey** which is like watery milk. Whey was used to preserve some food. The Vikings drank beer and wine. They also made a drink called **mead** from honey and water, and drank buttermilk which is the thin milk left over when cream is turned into butter.

△ Beer was drunk from drinking horns. These were usually made from cows' horns. They were hollowed out and the rim was trimmed with a metal band. Rich Vikings had drinking-horns made of gold or silver. These had bands of pattern from top to bottom. The shape of the horn made it impossible to put it down until it was empty. This meant all the beer had to be drunk at once or the horn passed on to someone else.

Eating a meal

The Vikings ate two main meals a day. The first was at about eight in the morning and the other at about seven at night. Trestle tables were set up in the hall. The benches around the walls could be used as seats. The Vikings also had fold-up chairs. The master of the house and his wife sat in the **high seat.** This was

◁ Iron cauldrons and tripods were used for cooking in Viking homes. The tripod stood over the fire, holding the cauldron just above the flames. Meat such as pork and ham was boiled in it. Stews were also made in it. Sometimes meat was baked in a deep pit filled with embers from the fire and covered with soil. Bread could also be baked this way. Some hearths had a flat stone slab across one end. This got very hot and bread could be baked on there, too. A house at Jarlshof, Shetland, had a stone oven which was partly built into a wall. Fish was cooked in this between two layers of grass with red-hot stones underneath and on top.

placed in the centre of the hall. At each side of it was a carved wooden post. Opposite was a similar seat for the main guest. Some food was served in wooden bowls and eaten with wooden spoons. Meat was eaten off a flat wooden dish, using fingers and a knife as there were no forks.

◁ This is some of the kitchen equipment found on the Oseberg ship. Most of it was made from wood, although there were metal bands around some of the containers. The drainer in the front of the picture next to the axe was used in making cheese. The curds were put in the top part and any remaining whey would run down into the bottom part.

Feasting and poetry

The Vikings had three main religious **feasts** each year. One was called *Sigrblot* and took place at the beginning of summer. The next was *Vetrarblot,* which was after the harvest. *Jolablot* was the third and took place after mid-winter. *Blot* means sacrifice and at each feast a horse was sacrificed to the gods. In exchange, the Vikings asked for rich harvests, mild winters and victory in battle.

After the horse had been dedicated to the gods, the Vikings cooked and ate its meat. They also ate beef and pork at their feasts, which sometimes lasted for two weeks. They drank plenty of strong thick ale and mead out of drinking-horns. The strong ale was brewed especially for the feasts. Rich Vikings drank wine from silver cups. There were white linen cloths on the tables and some families owned silver spoons and dishes, decorated with gold.

Vikings often travelled a long way to go to a feast at the home of a relation or friend. When they arrived, they hung up their weapons and shields. They wore their best clothes. One Viking in *Njal's Saga,* wore 'a blue tunic with a silver belt, blue striped trousers and black top boots'. He also combed his hair back from his forehead and held it there with a silk band.

After the meal was eaten, the entertainment started. Much of this was based on the spoken word. Poets, or *skalds,* made up new verses or recited old ones. These poems contained many *kennings,* which described an object without saying what it was. For example, a ship could be 'an ocean-striding bison' and a sword could be 'a battle adder'. Other people told riddles and swapped verses. The old sagas were repeated and new stories invented.

One famous skald was Egil Skallagrimsson. He made an enemy of Eirik Bloodaxe, king of Norway. Eirik later became king of York and Egil visited him there. Eirik's wife wanted Egil to be put to death at

△ The best skalds travelled round, making up verses, or drapa, praising their hosts. If the host liked the *drapa,* the skald was rewarded with a generous gift, such as this silver armlet.

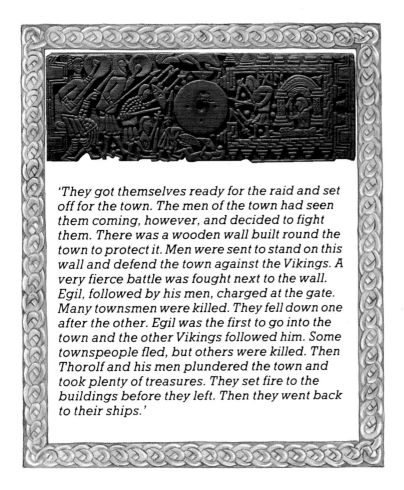

'They got themselves ready for the raid and set off for the town. The men of the town had seen them coming, however, and decided to fight them. There was a wooden wall built round the town to protect it. Men were sent to stand on this wall and defend the town against the Vikings. A very fierce battle was fought next to the wall. Egil, followed by his men, charged at the gate. Many townsmen were killed. They fell down one after the other. Egil was the first to go into the town and the other Vikings followed him. Some townspeople fled, but others were killed. Then Thorolf and his men plundered the town and took plenty of treasures. They set fire to the buildings before they left. Then they went back to their ships.'

◁ *Egil's Saga* tells of Egil's many Viking adventures in Iceland, Norway and England. He and Thorolf often went raiding together in their two longships. This extract from *Egil's Saga* tells of what happened on one of these raids.

△ A picture of Egil Skallagrimsson from a seventeenth century manuscript of *Egil's Saga*. This tells the story of three generations of Egil's family. Besides being a skald, Egil was a Viking warrior. He made up this verse when he was a child:
'My mother once told me, She'd buy me a longship, A handsome-oared vessel To go sailing with Vikings: To stand at the stern-post And steer a fine warship, Then head back for harbour And hew down some foemen.'

once. Eirik promised to spare him only if he could write a *drapa* of 20 verses in praise of Eirik. Egil managed to do this overnight. The poem was called *The Head Ransom* and Egil's reward was his own life.

There was also music, but little evidence of this remains. A set of **pan pipes** made from wood, and part of a stringed instrument were found in York. The sagas mention harps and fiddles. Dancing took place to the sound of verse-singing. The Arab trader Al-Tattushi did not have a high opinion of the voices at Hedeby. He wrote, 'I have never heard a more horrible singing. It is like a growl coming out of their throats, like dogs barking, only much more beastly.'

Sports and games

Falconry, or hunting with birds of prey, was a popular sport among the Vikings. They trained hawks and eagles as well as falcons to hunt and kill other wild birds and animals. Dogs were also trained to go on the hunt and collect whatever the hawks killed. These dogs were greatly valued and laws were set out to say how much money had to be paid if one Viking killed another's dog.

The Vikings also loved their horses and often mentioned them in the sagas. In the *Ynglinga Saga,* for example, a horse called Hrafn is described as 'black as midnight, with hooves as bright as stars'. As well as hunting on horseback, the Vikings organized horse races and horse fights. Horse fighting was a popular sport with the Vikings.

Wrestling was another sport the Vikings enjoyed taking part in and watching. It usually took place on a level field with a pointed stone, called the wrestling stone, in the middle. The audience stood around the edges, watching each of the two wrestlers trying to force the other one to the stone.

▽ A scene from the Bayeux tapestry, showing a wealthy man out hunting. *St Olaf's Saga* explains how the hawk and the dogs were used to catch wild birds. It describes how 'King Olaf rode out early with his hawks and dogs. When they let the hawks loose, the king's hawk killed two woodcocks in one flight. Then the hawk flew forward again and killed three more. The dogs followed them and caught every bird that fell to the ground.' Although the hawks were fierce birds, they were trained to obey their owners and to come back to them.

In summer many outdoor sports reflected the Vikings' love of the sea. These sports included rowing, sailing and swimming, with competitions to see who could stay underwater longest. Children took part, as well as adults. In winter, they played ball-games on frozen lakes and rivers and went skiing and skating for pleasure. Even kings did this. In the *Heimskringla,* King Eystein says to his brother, King Sigurd, 'I was so skilful on skates that I knew no one could beat me, and you could no more skate than an ox'.

In warmer weather, Vikings enjoyed running, jumping, shooting with bows and arrows, fencing, rock-climbing and lifting heavy weights or stones. Balancing competitions were also popular. The most famous of these was won by Olaf Tryggvason who walked the length of his warship and back by stepping from one oar to the next as the men rowed. Many of these sports were also good training for the Viking warrior who would also need strength and speed to survive in battle.

▽ These carved chess pieces are from the Viking Age. They were found on the Isle of Lewis in the Hebrides. Viking traders probably first saw chess played in Arabia and brought the game back home with them. Chess was known in Iceland in the twelfth century and chess pieces have been found there, as well as in Sweden, Dublin and York. The Vikings also had a game which used dice and peg-boards. In Ballinderry, Ireland, a board was found with 49 holes and little bone pegs to move round in them. None of the rules have survived, however, and so it is not known how these games were played.

The port of Birka

The Vikings travelled by ship to other countries and brought goods back home with them. These Viking traders needed markets where they could show the items they had for sale. At first they used temporary stalls which could be taken down when everything had been sold. As trade increased, however, the traders had more goods to sell. The stalls needed to be there every day. Towns started to grow around the markets. Craftsmen moved in and some traders built warehouses for their goods. Landing places were built so that ships could be unloaded more easily.

As these trading towns became richer, there was a danger that they would be attacked by enemy armies or raided by other Vikings. To protect towns from these attacks, wooden stockades were built around

▽ Birka was a busy port all year round. In winter the lake froze and fur traders could cross it on skates or sledges. In summer ships came in to unload on the waterfront or in one of the three harbours: People from many countries mixed in the streets, buying and selling goods.

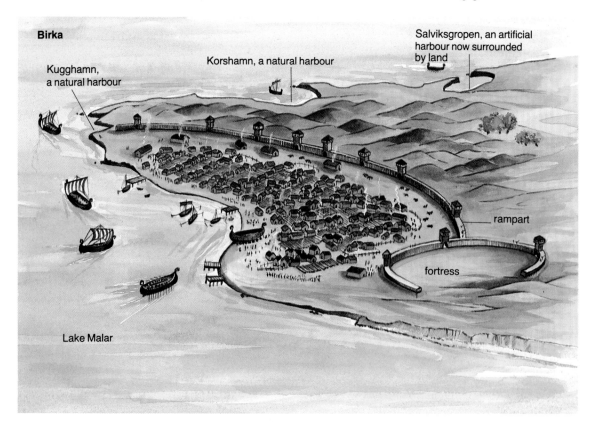

Birka

Kugghamn, a natural harbour

Korshamn, a natural harbour

Salviksgropen, an artificial harbour now surrounded by land

rampart

fortress

Lake Malar

◁ An aerial view of Birka. Part of the trading centre was in the foreground bordered by a rampart. On the hilly ground outside the rampart was a fort and the burial grounds. Since the Viking Age, the land has risen. This changed the shape of Birka's harbours.

the harbours. Earth was piled up into **ramparts** around the towns to protect them from attacks from the land. These ramparts were topped with a strong wooden fence and had gates to allow people in and out.

Much of the evidence comes from excavations in market towns which were abandoned in Viking times. One of these was Birka in Sweden. It was on an island in Lake Malar where water routes from the south and east met. Birka became a market in around 800 and after only a short time about 1000 people lived there. Evidence of industries such as leather-working and bronze-casting has been found. Houses have also been excavated. Some of these were made of wooden planks, or **staves.** Others had walls made of **wattle-and-daub.** This is made from twigs woven together and covered in clay to keep the water out.

From excavations at Hedeby, Denmark, we know that many of these town houses were similar to longhouses. They stood in fenced-off plots at right angles to the streets. Many plots also had a storehouse or a workshop and a well for water. The streets also ran at right angles to each other. Unfortunately not enough of Birka has been excavated to know if the streets there followed the same pattern.

Crafts and trades

Although the Viking farmer made most of the things his family needed, some were made by special **craftsmen.** Many of these craftsmen lived in the trading centres where there were plenty of people to buy their products. Evidence from Hedeby shows that their workshops were spread throughout the town and not just concentrated in one place. The blacksmiths were the only craftsmen who worked together in one area. They were mostly near the edge of the town because of the danger of fire spreading from their **furnaces.**

The blacksmiths made tools and weapons from iron. Some of this metal was found in marshes and bogs, but better quality iron was also imported. Other metalworkers made jewellery from bronze, silver and pewter. Their most popular items were the many brooches which all Vikings wore. Bronze brooches were made in clay moulds. Bronze is a mixture of copper and tin. The metals have to be so hot that they melt before bronze can be made into different

◁ This section of a horse's harness was found in Denmark. The metal-work was cast in bronze and then gilded, or covered in a thin layer of gold. To make the gold sparkle in the sun, tiny notches were carefully cut into the raised lines of the pattern. This was known as chip-carving. Sometimes a metal of a different colour was inlaid into a design to make the pattern more obvious. This was done especially on iron, when a pattern would be cut into the piece of iron and then filled with molten silver. Silver objects were decorated with niello. This was a pattern cut into the metal and filled with a black mixture containing sulphur.

shapes. When the hot metal had set, the brooch could only be removed by breaking the clay mould. This meant a new mould had to be made for each bronze brooch. Brooches of pewter could be cast in moulds of bone or stone. Pewter is a mixture of lead and tin. This softer metal can be shaped when it is warm. The moulds were in two halves and opened to take the brooch out. Brooches made out of pewter were much cheaper because these moulds could be used time after time.

Other craftsmen made pendants, dice and gaming pieces from **amber** and **jet.** Jet was only found near Whitby in England but there was amber in both Sweden and Denmark. Amber was made into beads for necklaces, too. Beads were also made from glass. The Vikings did not make glass of their own and so it was imported from Germany in small pieces. These came in many colours. Some beads were just one colour, but many patterned ones have also been found.

Bone carvers made objects from the antlers of deer. They carved pins and spoons, as well as combs. Other craftsmen worked in wood to produce cups and bowls, barrels and stools. Leather-workers made shoes and boots. Many of these goods were sold in the towns where they were made. Others were sold to **merchants** who took them round the remote farms to sell them again.

△ The tools of a blacksmith from Norway. The base of the anvil and the handles of the two hammers in the middle are made of new wood. The old wood had rotted away. Everything else is original. The shears under the hammers would be used for cutting metal. The tongs on the right would be used for holding moulds full of molten metal or for bending metal rods while they were still hot. The metal plate on the left with holes in would be used for making iron nails. In Sweden a set of carpenter's tools survived after it had been lost in a marsh in the Viking Age.

◁ Throughout the Viking world the antlers of red deer were used for making combs. The antlers were collected from the countryside after the deer had shed them in the spring.

Merchant adventurers

Our knowledge of Viking trade routes comes from many sources. In towns such as Hedeby and Birka, rich merchants had some of their goods buried with them in their graves. Archaeologists have excavated some of these and found out where the various items came from. Craftworkers in the towns imported some of their raw materials, too. These included glass and jet for beads.

Rune-stones also give us evidence of the Viking trade routes and are important in two ways. First there are rune-stones in the Vikings' homelands which mention journeys made by the Vikings. Then there are runes which the Vikings carved in other countries. A Swedish traveller carved some letters on a stone statue of a lion in a harbour in Greece. The lion is now in Venice, Italy. There is also a carving in runes in Hagia Sophia church in Istanbul, Turkey.

The sagas also tell stories of merchants and their journeys. In *Egil's Saga* we read that 'Thorolf put dried fish, skins and furs on board his ship and sent it

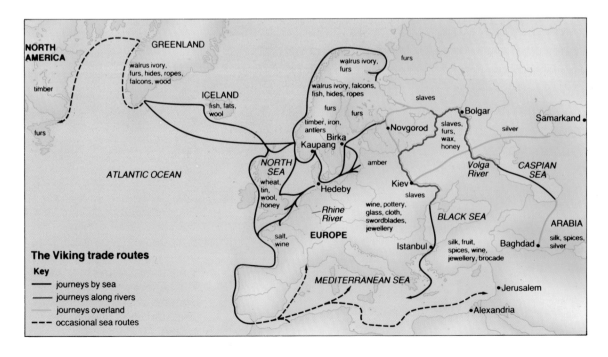

The Viking trade routes

Key
— journeys by sea
— journeys along rivers
— journeys overland
--- occasional sea routes

◁ The early Vikings did not have coins of their own. Instead, they exchanged their goods for different goods of a similar value or for a weight of silver. This silver was often in the form of coins from as far away as Samarkand and Arabia, beyond the Caspian Sea. The silver was also in small bars or ingots and in hack-silver. These were pieces which had been cut from coins or from jewellery to make up a certain weight.

△ The Viking method of buying and selling meant that a trader had to carry a set of weighing-scales around with him. These were made of bronze and folded up to fit in a special box or a pouch. As the units of weight were only small, the scale-pans were between five and seven centimetres across. Once kings became established in the Vikings' homelands, however, coins were minted and the old system of weighing silver slowly disappeared.

westwards to England. They found a good market, loaded their ship with wheat and honey, wine and cloth and returned home in the autumn.'

Ibn Fadlan and Ibn Rustah wrote about the slaves the Vikings transported along the Volga River in the tenth century. These slaves were taken to Bolgar or to Istanbul, which the Vikings called Miklagard. In these markets, the slaves were exchanged for Arab silver and luxury goods such as silk and spices from the east. King Alfred of Wessex, in England, wrote about a Norwegian called Ottar who visited England in the late ninth century. Ottar brought with him bearskins, ropes made out of walrus hide, and feathers for stuffing pillows and quilts.

There was also trade between the Vikings' homelands and the places they settled. For example, Iceland had few trees but plenty of fish. Therefore timber from western Norway was sent to Iceland in exchange for dried fish. Not every merchant arrived with his cargo, however. There was always the danger of a shipwreck. There was also the threat of an attack from Viking pirates who were more interested in raiding than trading.

Transport

When the Vikings travelled, they liked to go by sea or along rivers in their boats. Not everywhere could be reached by boat, however, so the Vikings had to go to some places overland. In Denmark this was fairly easy. The land was flat and the Romans had built good roads there a few hundred years before. In Norway and Sweden overland travel was more difficult, as there were forests and mountains to cross. There were also marshes, and special roads had to be built across them. These roads were sometimes known as bridges and many can still be seen in Sweden today. Some have rune-stones to say who built them. At Laby, near Uppsala, there are two rune-stones which read, 'Jarl and Karl and Jokulbjorn had this bridge made in memory of their father, Jofur'. Another rune-stone in Hadeland reads, 'Gunnvor, Thirdrik's daughter, made this bridge in memory of her daughter, Astrid; she was the most skilful maiden in Hadeland'.

△ ◁ Viking skates were made from the smoothed foot bones of horses and cattle. The boot rested on the skate and could be tied to it by a strip of leather from a peg in a hole at the front or back of the skate. The feet were never lifted from the ice because skaters pushed themselves along with poles.

◁ This wooden wagon from the Oseberg ship burial is similar to those on the tapestry (below). The bodies of the wagons could be taken off the wheels and some have been found used as coffins for wealthy women in southern Scandinavia. This one is richly decorated for its royal owner, but plainer ones would be in everyday use.

Methods of travelling

Travelling overland was often easier in the winter when the lakes and rivers were frozen. This meant people could skate from one place to another. Many skates have been found at excavations as far apart as York in England, and Staraya Ladoga in the USSR, as well as in the Vikings' homelands. Evidence of **snowshoes** and skis have been discovered and skis are mentioned in the sagas. For instance, in the *Orkneyinga Saga,* Earl Rognvald says, 'I glide on skis'. Sledges have also been found and these would be used for carrying heavy loads over snow and ice.

In the summer, rich Vikings travelled on horseback. People who could not afford a horse had to walk. Where there were suitable roads, heavy loads were carried by pack-horses or on horse-drawn wagons. There were also sledges which could run over grass and these were used where there were no roads. Much was learned about overland transport from the ship burial at Oseberg, where finds included a saddle, harnesses, carts, sledges and the bones of horses.

△ A reconstruction of part of the Oseberg tapestry shows horse-drawn wagons in a procession. Nobody is certain whether these scenes are from everyday life or if they are part of a story. Whoever designed them, however, probably based them on things they had seen.

Ships and shipbuilding

The Vikings' greatest achievement was in shipbuilding. At a time when other Europeans hardly dared to sail out of sight of land, the Vikings crossed the Atlantic Ocean. They also travelled long distances inland along rivers and landed at places where there were no harbours. This was possible because of the special design of Viking ships. The smallest one held four men and was known as a *faering.* The raiders sailed in ships known as longships, which were long and narrow. Merchants sometimes used these, too. They also used ships called *knarrs.*

All these ships were similar in design. They were long and slender with a high curve at each end. They were light enough to sail in very shallow water, but also strong enough to survive a storm. This was because they were flexible and would bend in a rough sea, rather than break up. The larger ships could be sailed or rowed. On inland journeys they could be picked up by the sailors and carried from

△ *A faering,* a four-oared boat which was found inside the Gokstad ship. It is 6.5 metres long and 1.4 metres wide.

△ An ocean-going trader, or *knarr,* from Roskilde. It is 16.3 metres long and 4.6 metres wide and more sturdily built than the coastal trader.

◁ The Gokstad ship was over 23.3 metres long and 5.2 metres broad. It was built mostly of oak, but had a pine mast. Its sail was made of strips of red and white cloth. It was steered by a large paddle fixed near the back of the ship on the starboard or right-hand side.

◁ The Oseberg burial ship. This is 21.6 metres long and 5 metres wide at its broadest point.

one river to another. Any sloping beach could be used for a landing.

Until the mid-1800s knowledge of Viking ships came only from the sagas and pictures carved on stones. Then the excavation of three ship burials in Norway added much to the archaeologists' knowledge. The first excavation was at Tune in 1867, but unfortunately much of the ship there had rotted away. Archaeologists were luckier at Gokstad in 1880 and Oseberg in 1903. The ships there had both been buried in blue clay and this had preserved them almost completely. These three were all longships, however. Then in 1962 evidence for merchant ships was found in the excavation at Roskilde, Denmark. As well as two longships, this revealed the remains of an ocean-going *knarr,* a coastal trader and a fishing boat or ferry.

◁ The ship from Gokstad, Norway. When it was excavated in 1880, it contained the body of a man in his fifties. He had been buried with his weapons and other possessions, including three small boats. Archaeologists have reconstructed the ship and models have also been made of it. One was sailed from Bergen to Newfoundland in 28 days in 1893.

Building a Viking longship

Ships were usually built in the winter when little other work could be done. They were often built in the open air, but sometimes they were built in a boatshed. The first job was to choose the oak trees. Ship builders used oak for almost every part of the ship. They needed one oak tree with a trunk about 18 metres long for the **keel**. The keel forms the base of the frame of the ship. The other tree trunks needed to be about five metres long. These were cut in half and half again along their length, rather like slicing a round cake. This produced the wedge-shaped planks for the sides of the ships. More timber was needed for the supports which held the ship in place while it was being built.

After the keel had been cut to shape and put on the supports, the front and the back posts were nailed to it. The planks were added, working from the bottom upwards. After this, the ribs which held the ship in shape were fixed to the planks. Then a strong block of wood was fixed to the keel in the middle of the ship to support the mast.

Clinker building

After the first line of planks had been fixed in place with iron nails, the second line was fastened above them. The wedge shape allowed this second line to overlap the first. This is known as clinker-building. It makes the ship flexible so that it can sail on rough seas without breaking up.

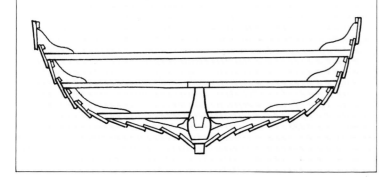

▷

Oarholes were cut into the top plank at each end of a merchant ship and along the full length of a longship.

The keel was the backbone of the ship. The two end posts were added onto each end to give the ship its curved shape. The planks, or strakes, were then fastened on, starting at the bottom and working upwards.

Timbers to make a frame and hold the ship in shape were added after the bottom planks were fixed in place. These timbers were attached to the planks and not to the keel.

Floor timbers were placed on top of the frame and fastened to the planks by wooden pegs. In longships the Vikings stood their sea chests on this floor and sat on them to row.

The mast block was fixed to the keel in the middle of the ship. It was a heavy block of wood with a slot in the middle for the mast to stand in. When the mast was in place, the mast block helped to spread the weight of the mast evenly across the ship.

The rudder on a Viking ship was like a large wooden paddle and was always near the stern on the starboard side of the ship.

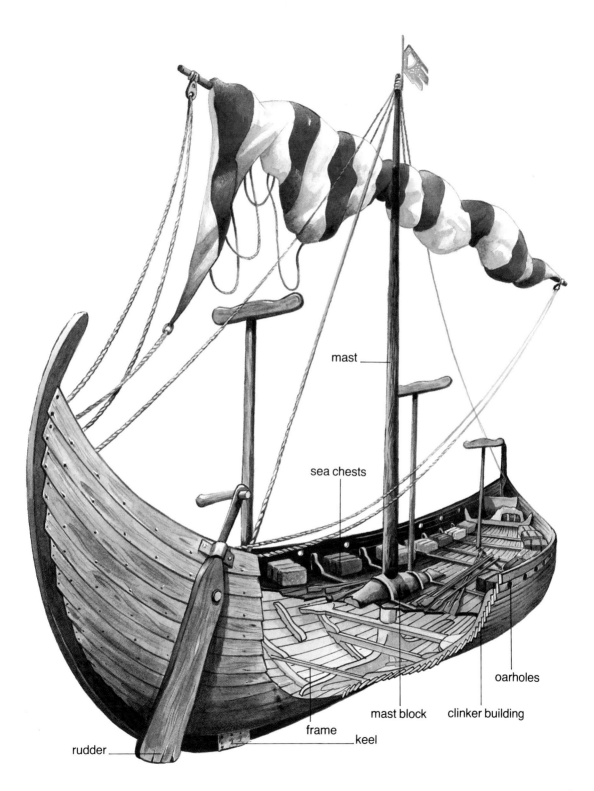

mast

sea chests

oarholes

mast block

clinker building

frame

keel

rudder

Sailing and navigation

Vikings sailed their ships when the wind was strong enough. If the wind dropped, however, the ship had to be rowed. No rowing benches have been found on the excavated ships, but the oar-holes are too low for men to row standing up. It is likely that the Vikings sat on the chests which they took to sea with them. These chests probably contained their weapons and some spare clothes. The clothes would be needed as it could get very cold and wet on the open deck of a Viking ship.

Food for the journey was stored under the small decks at each end of the ship. It would include vats of butter and cheese and barrels of beer, water and sour milk. There would be sacks of apples and nuts and also casks of meat and fish which had been dried, smoked or salted.

Also stored on board the ship were large **awnings** to make a shelter, and some tent-posts. When the ship was in harbour, the tent posts were put up on deck and the awnings were stretched between them. They protected the ship and people on board from the rain and the sun.

When the Vikings were sailing close to the coast, they sometimes landed their ship on a beach for the night. The awnings were taken ashore and set up as tents. The men brought their sleeping bags off the ship and put them in the tents. They also brought the ship's big cooking pot and made themselves a hot meal.

On long voyages across the open sea, however, they had to sleep on board. They usually had to eat cold food, too, although sometimes cooking was done on board. The cooking fire was contained in a box of sand so it could not set the wooden ship alight.

No one is certain how the Vikings found their way on the open sea. When there was no land in sight, they must have relied on watching the sun and the

△ A scene from one of the Gotland stones, showing a Viking ship in full sail. Many of these stones show a diamond pattern on the sail, but the sagas speak of sails with vertical stripes. It is possible that this pattern is supposed to represent ropes on the sail, as quite a lot of rope was found with the sail on the Gokstad ship. Also found on the Gokstad ship were yellow and black shields. These could be hung over the sides of the ship to protect the rowers or for display when the ship was in harbour. There were also wooden bailers and a bucket for emptying sea water out of the ship in rough weather.

◁ This gilded bronze weather-vane from Söderala in Sweden was originally fixed on the top of the mast of an eleventh-century Viking ship. Streamers or metal pendants would have been attached through the series of holes on the lower edge to blow and rattle in the wind. Some of these vanes have survived beyond the end of the Viking Age because they were removed from the ships and used again on churches.

stars. They also passed on directions to each other. The *Landnamabok* tells how to get from Norway to Greenland. 'From Hernar keep sailing west to Hvarf. Sail north of Shetland so you just see it in very clear weather, but south of the Faeroes so the sea appears halfway up the mountains. Then south of Iceland so you see the birds and whales from there.'

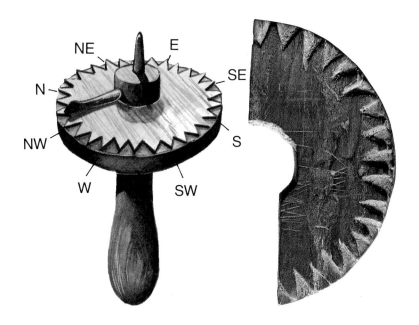

◁ The broken disc of wood on the right, was found in 1948 in the ruins of a settlement in Osterbygden, Greenland. It was probably part of a bearing-dial, like the reconstruction on the left. The dial has 32 compass points. The sun would cast a shadow from the pin onto the dial. The Vikings would then know in which direction they were sailing.

Raiders and traders

The Viking Age started towards the end of the eighth century when the Vikings began to travel overseas. To find out why they went, however, we must first look at the seventh century.

During the seventh century much more iron was being found in the bogs and marshes. This meant that more iron tools could be made and these were used to cut down trees and clear more land for farming. This led to more food being produced and so people were better fed and healthier than they had been in the past. More babies and children lived to be adults and this increase in population began to cause problems.

By tradition, only the eldest son of a Viking family inherited the family farm. The other sons had to look for farms of their own. At first they could clear more land and farm on that. By the end of the eighth century, however, there was no longer enough good

▽ Two pages from the *Codex Aureus,* a manuscript stolen by the Vikings during a raid on Kent. A man called Earl Alfred paid the Danes for the manuscript and brought it back to England. He wrote about this in Anglo-Saxon in the margin of one page. Translated, it reads, 'I, Earl Alfred, and Werberg my wife, have acquired this book from a heathen army with our true money, that is, with pure gold, and this we have done for the love of God and for the good of our souls, and because we are not willing that this holy book shall remain any longer in heathen hands'.

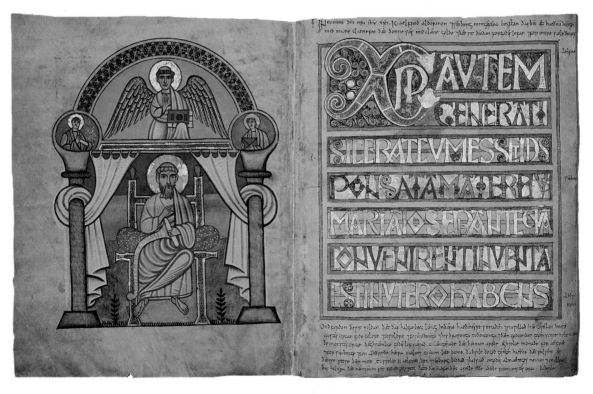

◁ Although most Vikings were farmers, there was a limited amount of farmland in their homelands. As this photograph shows, Norway is very mountainous with narrow fjords going a long way inland. The fjords have fertile farmland along their shores, but there is not very much of it. As the population began to expand, there was not enough farmland for everyone. There were similar problems in Sweden where much of the land was either marshy or thickly forested, and in Denmark where there were large areas of sandy heathland where nothing would grow.

farmland in the Viking homelands and younger sons had to find other ways of making a living.

The eighth century saw changes in other parts of Northern Europe, too. Stronger kings came to power and ended quarrels within their kingdoms. People began to enjoy peaceful times. Trade increased and more goods were transported across the seas. The Vikings had better ships and many Vikings now saw their chance to make a living as traders or pirates or both.

Some also went raiding. In 787, the Anglo-Saxon Chronicle records three boatloads of Vikings came to Dorset, on the South coast of England, in the reign of King Brihtric and killed the servant he sent to meet them. Then, on 8 June 793, came the raid on the monastery at Lindisfarne, on the north east coast. Simeon of Durham described it as follows.

'(The Vikings) laid everything to waste with grievous plundering, trampled the holy places with dirty feet, dug up the altars and seized all the treasures of the holy church. They killed some of the brothers. Some they took away with them in chains. Many they drove out, naked and loaded with insults, and some they drowned in the sea.'

Viking warriors

The Vikings were fearless warriors. They had a saying, 'No man limps while both his legs are the same length'. In spite of this bravery, they relied on surprise for their early victories. This was because the Vikings were usually much smaller in number than the people they were fighting against. If the other side started to overwhelm them, the Vikings would fight together from behind a wall made from their shields. Otherwise they preferred to fight hand to hand using their favourite weapons. These were the battle-axe and the sword.

If they were in a planned, or **pitched battle** on land, the Vikings started by firing showers of arrows onto their enemies. Then they threw spears. This is described in the Anglo-Saxon poem, *The Battle of Maldon*. 'They let the spears ... fly from their hands. Bows were busy. Point pierced shield. The rush of battle was fierce. Warriors fell on both sides.' After this, however, the hand to hand fighting would start in earnest.

▽ Viking warriors believed they would need their weapons in Valhalla and so they were buried with them. Many swords have survived. So have axe-heads and spear-points, though their wooden handles have rotted away.

◁ The ring-mail shirt, or *byrnie,* was made from thousands of hand-made iron rings, all linked together. It was very expensive and so only a Viking leader could afford one. *Byrnies* were passed down from father to son.

◁ The shield was made of flat planks of wood, which were joined together edge to edge. The boss in the centre was made of iron. Sometimes there was also an iron rim around the edge of the shield.

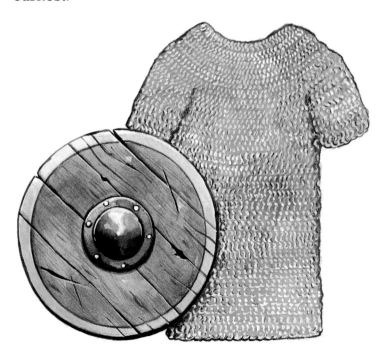

▷ The Viking sword was made of iron and often decorated with gold and silver. Many swords were made entirely by Viking blacksmiths. Others had imported blades which were made into complete swords by Viking craftsmen.

▷ The battle-axe had a blade which was about 24 centimetres across. This was mounted on a wooden shaft about 1.25 metres long.

▷ The spear was made of a metal point fixed on top of a long wooden shaft. Spears were usually thrown at the enemy at the start of a battle and picked up afterwards.

Battles at sea were much the same. Ships were lashed together so they could not be split up by the enemy. The chief warrior on each ship would stand in the front, or prow, and fight until he fell. Then he would be replaced. This chief warrior was often a brave fighter, called a *berserker.* These were very fierce Vikings. They got into a frenzy before a battle. Some were said to chew their shields. Others fought bare-chested. They were also said not to feel pain and could kill many men at a time.

Most Viking warriors were also farmers. Usually their reward for fighting was a share of the treasure. Sometimes, however, their leader was given money called ***Danegeld*** as a bribe to go away. He shared this with his men.

In Denmark the sites of four possible army **barracks** have been excavated. One is at Trelleborg where one of the buildings has been reconstructed. The sites date from the late tenth century. This may be where the army met before leaving for battle.

△ One of the Viking's most treasured possessions was his sword. Some have been found in graves. Archaeologists now know how they were made. The centre of the blade was made of several iron rods, twisted together while they were hot. They were then hammered flat. This made the blade strong and flexible. The cutting edges were of better quality iron and were welded to the blade. The handle, or hilt, was also iron, but was decorated with gold and silver. The sword was used to slash at the enemy, rather than stab. Some swords were thought to be magic and passed from father to son. They had names such as Leg-Biter and Adder.

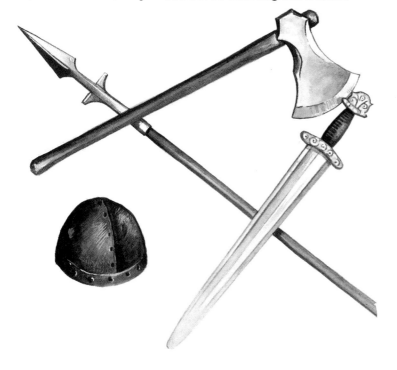

◁ Many Viking helmets were made of leather and fitted close to the head like a cap. Others were made of iron. The nose-guard was sometimes decorated, but the helmets never had horns or wings attached.

The Vikings in England

After the attack on Lindisfarne, little is known of the Vikings in England until 835. Then they attacked the Isle of Sheppey near the mouth of the River Thames. Fifteen years of raids followed. At this time, Vikings carried out their raid then went back home with whatever they had stolen. In 850, however, they stayed in England over the winter for the first time. In 865 the people of Kent paid *Danegeld* to the Vikings in exchange for a promise of peace. In 866 a 'great army' of Vikings arrived in England looking for land to settle on. Having conquered East Anglia, they moved on to York, in Northumbria. They captured the city and put a king of their own choosing on the throne of Northumbria. By 877 the whole country was in danger of attack by the Vikings.

In 878 the Vikings attacked Wessex, the most powerful of the seven kingdoms of England. Alfred was king of Wessex. He defeated the Vikings at Edington and made their leader, Guthrum, become a Christian. He also made Guthrum promise to keep his followers in just one part of England. This area became known as the **Danelaw.** Alfred then began to reclaim the other kingdoms from the Vikings. When he died in 899, only Northumbria and the *Danelaw* were still in Viking hands.

When Alfred died, his son Edward became king. Edward recaptured the *Danelaw,* but the Vikings held Northumbria. The last Viking king to rule in York was Eirik Bloodaxe. He was defeated in 954 and the whole of England was then ruled by one king.

In 978 Ethelred became king of England. The Vikings saw his weaknesses and soon demanded more and more *Danegeld.* By 1002 Ethelred was desperate. He ordered the killing of all Vikings in England. This made Svein Forkbeard, king of Denmark, even more determined to capture England. In 1013 he succeeded, but he died a few weeks later.

△ This cross is just one example of the Viking influence in the north of England. Stone crosses with carvings in Viking style are found in many churchyards in Yorkshire and Cumbria. One of these, at Middleton, Yorkshire, shows a Viking warrior, complete with his weapons. Others have scenes from both the Christian and Viking religions, like this one at Gosforth, Cumbria. Many place-names there and in the part of England that was called the *Danelaw* come from the Vikings, too. Some examples are Grimsby, Whitehaven, and Langtoft. 'By' meant a village, 'haven' was a harbour and 'toft' meant a building or farm. In the north of England, people still say 'dale' for valley, 'beck' for stream and 'tarn' for a pond. Words from the Vikings which have now been included in the English language are: egg, bread, lump and scrawny.

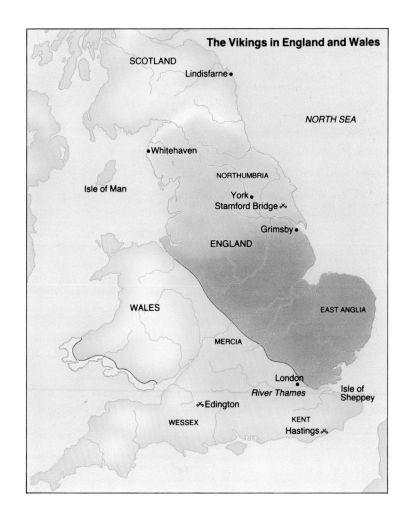

The Vikings in England and Wales

After Ethelred's death in 1016, Svein's son, Canute ruled Norway as well as England and Denmark. When Canute's son died in 1042, however, the English chose Ethelred's son, Edward the Confessor, as king. He died childless in 1066 and Harold Godwinson was chosen to replace him. The Norwegian Harald Hardradi attacked England, but Harold Godwinson defeated him at Stamford Bridge. Three days later an army from Normandy invaded England. Harold Godwinson hurried south, but was defeated at Hastings. Duke William of Normandy, a cousin of Edward the Confessor, became king and the Viking raids ended.

△ A rune-stone from Uppland, Sweden, in memory of Ulf, who 'received Danegeld three times in England. The first was paid by Tosti. Then Thorkel paid. Then Canute paid.'

Scotland and Ireland

In 795 Vikings from the Orkneys and the Hebrides sailed down the west coast of Scotland and raided the islands of Skye and Iona. Then they raided monasteries on islands off the coast of Ireland. This is recorded in Irish history and is the first written evidence of the Vikings in either Scotland or Ireland. Archaeological evidence also shows that by 800 some Norwegian Vikings had settled in the Orkneys and Shetlands. An excavation at a ninth-century farmstead in the Orkneys revealed a family cemetery. The men were buried with their weapons and had been warriors as well as farmers.

From these bases off Scotland, some Norwegian Vikings moved to the Scottish mainland and settled there. Others made more raids on Ireland. At first these were on the coast, but by 830 they went inland, up the rivers.

Then in 841 the Vikings started to build bases, called *long-phorts*, where they could stay over winter. The first was Dublin and it soon attracted merchants and craftsmen. Other *long-phorts* were built at Limerick, Cork, Wexford and Waterford. At the same time Danish Vikings came to Ireland. They joined forces with the Irish and in 851 defeated the Norwegians. Later that year the Norwegians recaptured Dublin and stayed there until 902. Then the Irish expelled them again.

Some Vikings then went back to Scotland. Others went to the Isle of Man and to north-west England. Around 912 they started raiding Ireland again and by 917 they were back in Dublin. This time they stayed and developed the settlement into a busy port. They expanded the other *long-phorts,* but they were not able to take much land for farming as the Irish people were already farming the land.

In 980 the Vikings were defeated by the Irish at Tara. This time the defeated Vikings were allowed to

△ Until the fifteenth century, the Shetlands were Norwegian islands. The Up-Helly-Aa festival held today in Lerwick, Shetland, remembers a Viking custom of burning a dead leader's body while his soul travels to Valhalla. The festival now takes place each year on the last Tuesday in January. A model Viking ship is dragged through the streets. It is followed by a procession of people carrying blazing torches. The leaders are dressed as Vikings. Eventually the ship stops in an open space and the torches are thrown onto the ship to set it on fire.

Other evidence of Vikings in Shetland is found in archaeological sites, such as Jarlshof, and in the many place names ending in 'wick', which meant a coastal market, 'ness' which meant a headland, and 'holm' which was Norwegian for island.

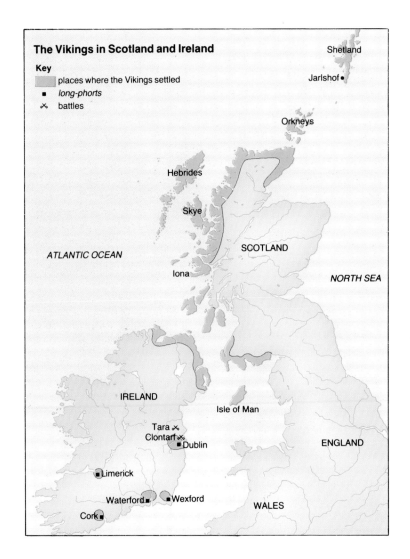

The Vikings in Scotland and Ireland

Key

▨ places where the Vikings settled
■ *long-phorts*
✕ battles

Shetland
Jarlshof •

Orkneys

Hebrides

Skye

ATLANTIC OCEAN

Iona

SCOTLAND

NORTH SEA

IRELAND

Isle of Man

Tara ✕
Clontarf ✕
■ Dublin

ENGLAND

■ Limerick

Waterford ■   ■ Wexford

WALES

Cork ■

stay, because they were skilled traders and their towns were very wealthy. The battles went on, however, and in 1014 the Vikings were defeated again, at Clontarf. Despite this, the Viking king, Sihtric Silkenbeard, ruled in Dublin for another 20 years. The Vikings stayed in their *long-phorts* and continued their trade. In 1170 an Anglo-Norman army attacked Dublin. These invaders were Normans whose families had settled in England 100 years before.

△ A section of woven wattle wall uncovered at the Wood Quay site in Dublin. Excavations also revealed an embankment running across the site. Built about 950, this embankment had been on the bank of the Liffey River. The river is now about 100 metres away.

France and the Mediterranean

From 768 to 814 the powerful King Charlemagne ruled France. He created a large **empire** beyond France. Some Vikings had traded with parts of this empire but in 810 Danish Vikings raided Frisia, on the North Sea coast. In 820 they tried again but were defeated. They also sailed into the mouth of the Seine River but were defeated there, too. In 834, however, the Vikings made a successful raid on Dorestad, a trading town by the Rhine River. More raids followed and in 845 the Vikings plundered Paris. The French king paid the Vikings 3000 kilograms of silver to leave his people in peace. That same year the Vikings reached Hamburg, in Germany. By 863 they had reached Cologne on the Rhine River.

At the same time Vikings from the Scottish islands attacked the Atlantic coast of France. In 835 they raided the monastery at Noirmoutier, an island at the mouth of the Loire River. Eight years later, the monks

◁ Arab armies took their Muslim religion to Spain in the eighth century. These Muslim soldiers were the first to defeat a large number of Vikings. This was in 844. The Vikings attacked north-west Spain, then sailed south. Some Vikings besieged Seville while others moved towards Cordoba. The people of Cordoba were expecting them, however, and had gathered an army together. This army ambushed the Vikings and defeated them. The Viking survivors left Spain and went back to France.

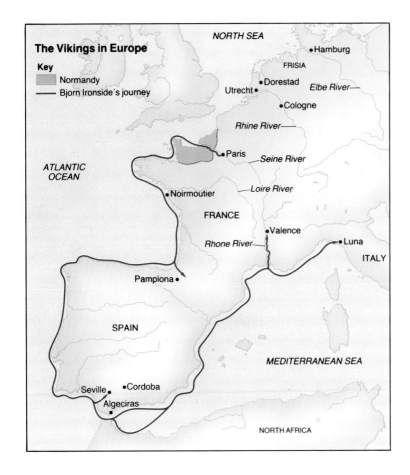

The Vikings in Europe

Key
- Normandy
- Bjorn Ironside's journey

NORTH SEA
• Hamburg
FRISIA
• Dorestad
Utrecht •
Elbe River—
• Cologne
Rhine River—
• Paris
Seine River
ATLANTIC
OCEAN
• Noirmoutier
Loire River
FRANCE
• Valence
Rhone River—
• Luna
ITALY
Pamplona •
SPAIN
MEDITERRANEAN SEA
Seville • • Cordoba
Algeciras
NORTH AFRICA

◁ In 859 Bjorn Ironside and Hastein were forced to leave the Isle of Jeufosse in the Seine River, near Paris. They headed for Spain with 62 ships containing gold, slaves and food. They sailed to Algeciras, in southern Spain, and burned the mosque. Then they crossed to North Africa and took some more slaves. After that they went to southern France and stayed for the winter. Next spring they looted the French town of Valence, 200 kilometres from the mouth of the Rhone River. Then they ransacked the town of Luna, Italy. In 861 they were again off the coast of Spain where they survived a sea-battle. They went on to Pamplona and held its prince to ransom. In 862 a third of the ships arrived back in France, landing at Noirmoutier with their loot.

had left and the Vikings made Noirmoutier into a winter base.

Rollo and Normandy

More and more *Danegeld* was paid to the Vikings, but they still kept on raiding. Then, in 911, the king of France, Charles the Simple, found a way of solving the problem. He made a treaty with a Viking chieftain called Rollo. The king promised to make Rollo the Duke of Normandy. In exchange Rollo had to promise to become a Christian and promise to defend Normandy against other Vikings. Rollo accepted this and he and his men settled in Normandy. Rollo married the king's daughter, Giselle.

△ This picture was drawn by a monk in the margin of a book called the *Utrecht Psalter*. It shows the monk's idea of what a Viking attack on a European city was like.

New lands to the west

Vikings from Norway first went to Iceland in about 860. There are stories about three different Vikings who saw the island first, but a Viking called Floki is the person who called it Iceland. The Vikings probably arrived by accident, because of a storm. Monks from Ireland already lived on Iceland, however. The writer of *Islendingabok,* or *Book of the Icelanders* in the twelfth century says that the monks left 'because they did not want to live with heathen men'.

Greenland

Greenland was probably first seen by a Viking called Gunnbjorn, who was blown off course between Norway and Iceland. This was about 920. In 980, however, Eirik the Red was outlawed from Norway because of 'some killings'. He went to Iceland, but was soon outlawed there, too. After three years in exile, he returned to Iceland to tell the settlers about Greenland. He chose this name because he thought it would make people 'much more eager to go there'. Around 985, 25 ships set sail from Iceland to follow him, but only 14 arrived in Greenland. The Vikings took animals with them from Iceland and there was plenty of fish in the sea, but corn, iron and timber had to be imported. All went well for about 200 years. Then the climate began to turn colder. Ice made the

△ This painting shows men catching a whale. The scene is painted within a letter on a page of a fourteenth century copy of the *Jonsbok.* This is the book of Icelandic laws. They date from the Viking Age.

◁ This reconstruction at L'Anse aux Meadows in Newfoundland is on the first genuine Viking site to be discovered in North America. Archaeologists found house foundations and the site of a smithy here during the 1960s. There were also some things made by Vikings, but no evidence to show that the Vikings lived there for very long. There have been attempts to forge evidence of Viking settlements in North America. In 1898 a rune-stone appeared in Kensington, Minnesota, but was proved to be a fake in 1958. Another forgery was the Vinland Map, published by Yale University in 1965. It was thought to have been drawn in about 1440. Later, however, the ink was analysed and found to contain a substance which was not in use before 1917.

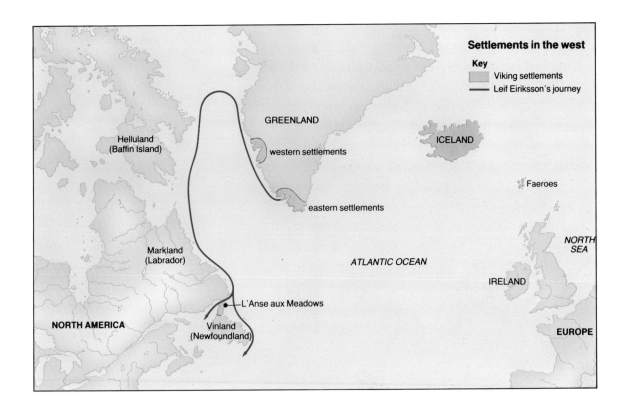

Settlements in the west

Key
- Viking settlements
- Leif Eiriksson's journey

GREENLAND

ICELAND

Helluland
(Baffin Island)

western settlements

eastern settlements

Faeroes

Markland
(Labrador)

ATLANTIC OCEAN

NORTH
SEA

IRELAND

L'Anse aux Meadows

NORTH AMERICA

Vinland
(Newfoundland)

EUROPE

seas dangerous and the merchants stopped visiting. Disease started to spread among the Vikings and by 1500 their farms were deserted.

North America

North America was also first seen by a Viking who was blown off course. This was Bjarni Herjolfsson in about 985. He did not land, however. Instead he returned to Greenland and told of what he had seen. Leif Eirikson went looking for this new land. He went first to Helluland, then to Markland and finally to Vinland. He stayed during the winter and returned to Greenland in the spring. His brother Thorwald went the next year, but was killed by the North American Indians. Later Thorfinn Karlsefni tried to settle in Vinland, but only stayed three years.

Trade routes to the east

Around 860, Vikings from Sweden went east across the Baltic Sea and the Gulf of Finland to Russia. The area they went to was already inhabited by tribes of Slavs. Most of the Slavs lived by farming and hunting. Some were traders, too, and they had started to build trading settlements. One of these was at Ladoga. The Vikings went there to trade, too.

Ladoga was on the shores of a huge lake. From there, Vikings could travel by boat to join the Volga River. This took them to Bolgar, which was on an important overland trade route from the east. At the market in Bolgar they could trade their slaves and furs, wax and honey for silver from Arabia and silk from China. Some Vikings sailed beyond Bolgar down the Volga River and across the Caspian Sea. They then left their boats and went by camel to Baghdad. There they also traded for silver, silk and spices.

Another route from Ladoga went south along the Volkhov River to Novgorod. This was another trading town developed by the Vikings. From there they sailed towards the Dnieper River. To get to this river, the Vikings had to lift their boats out of the water and transport them overland. They did this either by carrying them or by rolling them on logs.

The Dnieper took the Vikings to Kiev. From there they always travelled on together in groups of ships. This was because of the stretch of dangerous rapids on the river beyond Kiev. The Vikings had to take their boats out of the water to pass the rapids and were then in danger of being attacked by local tribesmen.

Once past the rapids, the Vikings sailed on to the Black Sea and Istanbul, which they called Miklagard. There they traded their goods for spices and wine, silks and jewellery. Most traders then made the journey back up the rivers to the market at Birka, in

△ This rune-stone is at Broby in Sweden. It was erected by a woman called Estrid in memory of her husband. The inscription says, 'He visited Jerusalem and died in Greece'.

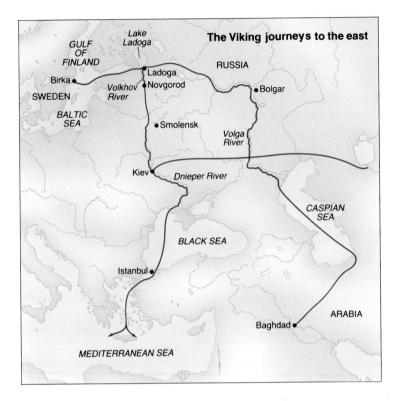

The Viking journeys to the east

Sweden. Others stayed behind, however. Some joined the Varangian Guard. These were the Viking soldiers who guarded the emperor in Istanbul. One of the most famous of these soldiers was Harold Sigurdson. He later became better known as Harald Hardradi, king of Norway from 1046 until 1066.

Ibn Fadlan described the burning or cremation of a dead Viking chief near the Volga River. The chief's body was dressed in new clothes, then 'they carried him to the tent on the ship. Beer, fruit and sweet-smelling plants were laid around him, together with bread, meat and onions.' Sacrifices of animals like hens or horses were made, then the ship and its contents were set on fire and burned to ashes. The contents of a warrior's grave at Gnezdovo on the Dnieper River confirm Ibn Faldan's description of a Viking funeral.

△ These finds are from a Viking settlement in Russia. The *Russian Primary Chronicle* says that the Slav tribes quarrelled fiercely among themselves. Then in 860 they asked the Vikings to send them a strong leader. A Viking called Rurik came from Sweden. The *Chronicle* says he founded the cities of Ladoga and Novgorod. Excavations at Ladoga and Novgorod, however, have revealed Slav settlements which are earlier than the Viking ones. Rurik also gave Russia its name, as the Slav name for the Vikings was Rus. Objects made by Vikings have also been found at Kiev and Smolensk.

The Viking sunset

There were many reasons why the Viking Age ended after 300 years. One was the spread of Christianity in the Vikings' homelands. Denmark was converted in the reign of Harold Bluetooth. Norway was next. Its first Christian king was Hakon the Good, but he was unable to convert many of his people before he died in 960. This was done by two later kings, Olaf Tryggvason and Olaf Haraldsson. After Olaf Haraldsson died in battle in 1030, people said miracles happened at his grave. He became known as Saint Olaf.

Sweden kept its old religion the longest. In the twelfth century a monk wrote, 'As long as things go well, they are willing to honour Christianity. When things go wrong, they revenge themselves on Christians and try to chase them out of the country'. Eventually Sweden was converted, however, and the Vikings' way of life had to change.

The **migrations** overseas stopped as farming methods improved in the Vikings' homelands. More land was brought into use and younger sons could get farms without moving overseas. In places like the

◁ King Harald Bluetooth of Denmark was baptised in a barrel of holy water. He was converted to Christianity in about 960 by a priest called Bishop Poppo. This golden altar-piece showing his baptism is from Tandrup Church in Denmark. Many Vikings in Norway, Denmark and Sweden were converted to Christianity by force. For them it meant giving up a way of life in which they made the rules and in its place accepting the rules of kings and bishops.

Danelaw, Russia and Ireland, Viking settlers married and mixed with the local population.

Raids went on into the twelfth century, but they were no longer successful. The rest of Europe was now ready for the Vikings and defeated them everywhere. Trading changed, too. Luxury goods were replaced by bulky goods. Bigger ships were needed and the Vikings lost their supremacy at sea.

The Viking legacy

An unexpected legacy from the Vikings is in law. The word law is Viking and the Vikings were the first people to use a jury of 12 ordinary men to decide who is right or wrong in a law case.

△ This smith's mould was used for Thor's hammers as well as Christian crosses. This was because the two religions existed side by side for a long time. Many Viking traders chose to become Christians. This made it easier for them to deal with other men who were already Christians. These Vikings kept their old religion as well, though. The Vikings in Iceland voted on religion in the year 1000. They decided to become Christian, but said the old religion could carry on in secret. Many Vikings must have been like Helgi the Lean. He 'believed in Christ, but prayed to Thor for sea journeys and emergencies'.

◁ The stave church at Borgund on the Sognefjord in Norway. 'Stave' means the walls are made of upright planks of wood. The inside of this church probably dates from the twelfth century. Much of the outside is from the thirteenth century. By this time the Viking Age was over, but the Viking influence was still there. Dragons as well as crosses were used for decoration on the roof.

Time line

789   The Vikings are first mentioned in the *Anglo-Saxon Chronicle* when they land on the south coast of England.

793   The Vikings raid the monastery at Lindisfarne, an island on the north-east coast of Britain.

795   The Vikings raid the Scottish island of Iona and make the first raids off the coast of Ireland.

800   By this date the Vikings had started to settle in the Orkney and Shetland Islands.

810   Danish Vikings raid Frisia.

814   Charlemagne dies and his French empire starts to collapse.

830s   Viking attacks on Ireland increase.

834   The Vikings raid the market town of Dorestad in the Netherlands.

835   Fifteen years of Viking raids on England start.

841   The Vikings build their first *long-phort* at Dublin in Ireland.

844   The Vikings reach Spain for the first time, but are defeated by the Arabs.

845   Ragnar Hairy-Breeches besieges Paris and is bought off with *Danegeld.*

850   The Vikings over winter in England for the first time. Swedish Vikings start to visit Russia.

851   The Norwegian Vikings are chased out of Dublin by the Danish Vikings and the Irish, but they reconquer Dublin later in the same year.

859   Bjorn Ironside sets out on his journey to the Mediterranean Sea.

860   Iceland is discovered by Norwegian Vikings. Swedish Vikings attack Istanbul.

866   The Great Army, led by the sons of Ragnar Hairy-Breeches, arrives in England.

867   The Danish Great Army captures York.

871   Alfred the Great becomes king of Wessex.

874   The first Vikings settle in Iceland.

878   Alfred the Great defeats the Vikings at the Battle of Edington.

885   Paris is besieged by another Great Army.

886   A treaty is drawn up by Alfred the Great to allow the Danish Vikings in England to settle in the *Danelaw.*

893   More Viking raids on England

899   Alfred the Great dies.

900   Harald Finehair becomes the first king of all Norway.

901   King Edward of Wessex starts to recapture England from the Vikings. When he dies in 924 he has succeeded in recapturing the country as far as the Humber River.

911   The king of France gives Normandy to the Viking leader, Rollo. He and his men start to settle there.

930   About 10 000 Vikings are living in Iceland. The first *Althing* meets there.

950   Fortresses such as Trelleborg start to be built in Denmark.

954   Eirik Bloodaxe, the last Viking king of York, is killed at the battle of Stainmore.

978   Ethelred the Unready becomes king of England.

980   Christianity starts to spread throughout the Vikings' homelands.

982   Eirik the Red sails from Iceland and reaches Greenland.

986   Bjarni Herjolfsson sees Vinland, but does not land.

991   Viking attacks start again on England. The Vikings win the Battle of Maldon. Much *Danegeld* is paid out from this year onwards.

995   Olaf Tryggvason becomes king of Norway.

1000   The people of Iceland decide to accept Christianity. Thorfinn Karlsefni travels to Vinland.

1002   Ethelred the Unready orders the killing of all the Danish settlers in southern England. Leif Eirikson sails from Greenland and reaches Newfoundland.

1009   Olaf the Stout attacks London and pulls down London Bridge.

1014   The Battle of Clontarf at which the Irish king Brian Boru defeats the Vikings in Ireland.

1016   Danish Vikings defeat the English at the Battle of Ashingdon. Svein Forkbeard becomes king of England but dies shortly afterwards and is followed by his son, Canute.

1030   Canute defeats and kills the Norwegian king Olaf Haraldsson at the Battle of Stiklarstad and becomes king of Norway, as well as Denmark and England.

1035   Canute dies and is followed by his son, Harthacanute.

1042   Harthacanute dies suddenly. Edward the Confessor is chosen to be king of England.

1047   Harald Hardradi becomes king of Norway.

1066   Edward the Confessor dies without an heir. Harold Godwinson is crowned king of England. Harald Hardradi invades northern England but is defeated and killed at the Battle of Stamford Bridge. Duke William of Normandy invades southern England and defeats Harold Godwinson at the Battle of Hastings. Duke William becomes King William I of England. The Viking raids finish.

1100   The end of the Viking Age.

Glossary

amber: a hard shiny, yellowish substance which is the fossilised resin of trees buried thousands of years ago

archaeologist: a person who learns about life in the past by looking for and studying objects from earlier times

artefact: an object which has been made by people

awnings: large pieces of strong waterproof cloth which could be made into tents or covers above the deck of a ship

barracks: a group of buildings where soldiers live

brocade: a cloth, usually made of silk, with a raised pattern woven onto it

byre: a building where farm animals live in the winter

ceremony: a formal occasion when events take place according to a set pattern

conquest: to gain, or win, something by force

craftsmen: someone who is skilled at a particular craft. For example, a carpenter

curds: the solid parts of milk, which separate out when milk sours or is heated to make cheese

Danegeld : money which the Vikings forced people to pay in order to be left in peace

Danelaw : the part of England allocated to the Vikings after being defeated by Alfred the Great. It included East Anglia, and five main towns: Derby, Leicester, Lincoln, Nottingham and Stamford

embroider: to decorate something, usually a piece of cloth, with needlework

empire: a group of countries which come under the control of one ruling country

excavation: the careful digging up of buried objects to find information about the past

falconry: using trained birds of prey to hunt and kill other wild birds and animals

feast: a large, rich meal held to celebrate something

feud: a long-lasting and violent quarrel between two families

flax: a type of plant whose stem fibres are woven into linen cloth

fodder: any plants which are grown for animal feed. For example, hay and straw

furnace: a very hot fire used by blacksmiths to heat metal so that it will bend

high-seat: the seat belonging to the owner of a Viking longhouse. The high-seat was always nearest to the fire, and had carved posts on either side of it

jet: a hard, black mineral very like coal but clean and shiny

keel: the main piece of wood that goes along the bottom of a ship from end to end

longhouse: a Viking farmhouse. It got its name because of its long, narrow shape

long-phort : one of the places in Ireland where the Vikings first stayed over winter. Later they developed into trading towns. Dublin was the most successful

mead: an alcoholic drink made from honey

merchant: a person who makes a living by travelling around the world, buying and selling goods

migration: to change your home from one area or country to another

monastery: a place where monks live and practise their religion

monk: a member of a group of religious men who live in monasteries away from the rest of the world

pan pipes: a musical instrument consisting of a set of different sized reeds or pipes fixed together, with their mouth pieces in line

pitched battle: a battle which is planned before it takes place, and is fought on a piece of land agreed by both sides

raider: a person who makes short and unexpected attacks, or raids, on other people and their property

rampart: a bank of earth built around a town to protect it from attackers

rune: one of the marks or letters used to write down the Viking language. Runes were straight and stick-like, which made them very easy to carve

sacrifice: the killing of an animal or person as an offering, usually to a god. Sacrifices were made by people to please the gods

saga: a long and detailed story of Viking adventures. The first sagas were written down in Iceland in the twelfth century

settler: a person who has left their homeland, and settles down to live in a new area or country

shieling: a meadow high up in the mountains for summer grazing but covered by snow in winter

shift: a simple loose-fitting dress, rather like a nightdress

smithy: a place where a blacksmith works

snowshoe: a light, oval wooden framework strung with thongs. Snowshoes are strapped to people's feet to stop them sinking into soft snow

soapstone: a type of rock which was quarried in Norway and Shetland

spit: a metal rod on which meat is skewered and roasted over the fire

staves: logs of wood which are split in two and stood on end in a row to make walls

stockade: a tall wooden barrier built around a place to protect it from attack

tapestry: a picture or design embroidered on canvas using different coloured wools. Viking Age tapestries often tell a story

thatch: a material such as straw, reeds and heather which is used to make a roof

trader: a person who makes a living by buying and selling goods

tunic: a loose garment worn on the upper half of the body. It usually reaches to the knees

Valhalla: the final home or paradise for dead Viking warriors

vellum: a specially prepared calf-skin which was used for writing on before paper was available

wattle-and-daub: a type of wall which is built by weaving twigs and branches together (wattle) and covering them with mud or clay (daub) to make the wall waterproof

whey: the thin part of milk left over when the curds have been removed

Index